I0425924

May 2012

MANAGING CRITICAL ISOTOPES

DOE's Isotope Program Needs Better Planning for Setting Prices and Managing Production Risks

GAO

Accountability ★ Integrity ★ Reliability

G A O
Accountability * Integrity * Reliability

Highlights

Highlights of GAO-12-591, a report to congressional requesters

May 2012

MANAGING CRITICAL ISOTOPES

DOE's Isotope Program Needs Better Planning for Setting Prices and Managing Production Risks

Why GAO Did This Study

DOE is the only domestic supplier for many of the over 300 different isotopes it sells that are critical to medical, commercial, research, and national security applications. Previous shortages of some isotopes, such as helium-3, an isotope used to detect radiation at seaports and border crossings, highlight the importance of managing supplies of and demand for critical isotopes. Prior reports by GAO and others highlighted risks and challenges faced by the Isotope Program, such as assessing demand for certain isotopes. GAO was asked to determine (1) which isotopes are produced, sold, or distributed either by the Isotope Program or NNSA and how the two agencies make isotopes available for commercial and research applications; (2) what steps the Isotope Program takes to provide isotopes for commercial and research applications; and (3) the extent to which DOE is assessing and mitigating risks facing the Isotope Program. GAO reviewed DOE and NNSA documents, visited Oak Ridge National Laboratory, and interviewed cognizant agency officials.

What GAO Recommends

GAO recommends, among other actions, that DOE's Isotope Program define what factors it considers when setting isotope prices, create clear objectives as a basis for risk assessment, and consolidate the lists of high-priority isotopes. DOE stated that it will address GAO's recommendations through the Isotope Program's current efforts to update its pricing policy and develop a strategic plan.

View GAO-12-591. For more information, contact Gene Aloise at (202) 512-3841 or aloisee@gao.gov.

What GAO Found

The Department of Energy's (DOE) Isotope Development and Production for Research and Applications program (Isotope Program) provides over 300 different isotopes for commercial and research applications. The Isotope Program is responsible for 243 stable isotopes that are no longer produced in the United States but are sold from the program's existing inventory and for 55 radioactive isotopes, called radioisotopes, that the program is able to produce at DOE facilities. An additional 10 isotopes sold by the Isotope Program are provided by the National Nuclear Security Administration (NNSA), a separate agency within DOE, as by-products of its nuclear weapons program.

The Isotope Program may be forgoing revenue that could further its mission because of the manner in which it sets prices for commercial isotopes. The Isotope Program determines demand, coordinates production, and sets prices for commercial isotopes. To set prices for radioisotopes, the program considers the full cost of production, including direct costs (e.g., labor costs) and indirect costs (e.g., infrastructure costs). For research applications, isotope prices are set to recover direct costs to reduce prices and encourage research. For commercial applications, prices are set at full cost recovery—of both direct and indirect costs—or at an isotope's market price when a market price higher than full cost recovery already exists. The program, however, has not fully assessed the pricing of most of these isotopes, as required by its 1990 pricing policy. This policy provides latitude for setting prices and states that prices should be assessed annually. Factors that may be considered when establishing prices include the value of an isotope to the customer, demand, and the number of suppliers. The program, however, has not assessed the value of isotopes to customers or defined what factors it will consider when it sets prices for commercial isotopes, including defining under what circumstances it will set prices at or above full cost recovery. As a result, the program does not know if its full-cost-recovery prices are set at appropriate levels so as not to distort the market, and it may be forgoing revenue that could further support its mission.

The Isotope Program has begun taking some actions to identify and manage risks to achieving its mission of producing isotopes, but because it has not established clear, consistent program objectives, the program's risk assessment efforts are not comprehensive. Actions the Isotope Program is taking include, among other things, identifying high-priority isotopes and using its revolving fund to mitigate risks from unforeseen events. For example, the Isotope Program has identified five lists of high-priority isotopes—those at risk of supply problems because they are already in short supply or are important to users. Isotope Program officials reported using these lists to set program priorities. The Isotope Program is taking these actions, however, without first establishing clear, consistent objectives. The federal standards for internal control state that a precondition to risk assessment is the establishment of clear objectives. Without clearly defined objectives, the program cannot be assured that it is assessing risks from all sources or that its efforts are focusing on the most significant risks to achieving its mission. Furthermore, without consolidating the multiple high-priority lists, Isotope Program managers may not be directing limited resources to the most important isotopes.

_____ United States Government Accountability Office

Contents

Abbreviations

DOE   Department of Energy
NNSA   National Nuclear Security Administration

United States Government Accountability Office
Washington, DC 20548

May 23, 2012

The Honorable Brad Miller
Ranking Member
Subcommittee on Energy and Environment
Committee on Science, Space, and Technology
House of Representatives

The Honorable Paul D. Tonko
Ranking Member
Subcommittee on Investigations and Oversight
Committee on Science, Space, and Technology
House of Representatives

The Department of Energy's (DOE) Isotope Development and Production for Research and Applications program (Isotope Program) is the only domestic supplier for many of the more than 300 different isotopes that it sells, many of which are critical to medical, commercial, research, and national security applications.[1] For example, the program produces and sells strontium-82, an isotope used to generate rubidium-82, which is used in the diagnosis of heart disease. Overall, approximately 20 million medical procedures are performed each year in the United States using isotopes. Other applications for isotopes include oil and gas exploration, physics research, and radiation detection monitors that screen cargo and vehicles at ports and border crossings. Additionally, a January 2012 federal workshop on isotopes was held by the Isotope Program and the National Nuclear Security Administration (NNSA), a separately organized agency within DOE,[2] to discuss isotope supply and demand. At this workshop, more than 20 federal government entities, including the Department of Defense's Defense Threat Reduction Agency, Department of Homeland Security's Domestic Nuclear Detection Office, National Aeronautics and Space Administration, National Institutes of Health, and

---

[1]Isotopes are varieties of a given chemical element with the same number of protons but different numbers of neutrons. For example, the helium-3 isotope has one less neutron than the helium-4 isotope, which is the helium isotope commonly used in party balloons.

[2]Congress created NNSA as a semiautonomous agency within DOE under Title 32 of the National Defense Authorization Act for Fiscal Year 2000 (Pub. L. No. 106-65, § 3211 (1999)). NNSA is responsible for the management and security of the nation's nuclear weapons, nonproliferation, and naval reactors programs.

GAO-12-591 DOE's Isotope Program

Federal Bureau of Investigation identified more than 100 different isotopes that are key to achieving their missions, according to program officials.

Previous shortages of some isotopes, such as helium-3, highlight the importance of managing supplies of and demand for critical isotopes. For example, in May 2011 we reported on a shortage of helium-3—an isotope used in radiation detection monitors deployed at ports and border crossings to detect nuclear material and prevent terrorists from smuggling such material into the United States.[3] DOE is the only domestic supplier of helium-3, producing about 8,000 liters per year. As demand for helium-3 increased beginning in 2001, sales quickly outpaced production levels, resulting in a critical shortage in 2008. As a result, the federal government was forced to quickly begin developing alternatives to helium-3 in order to continue deploying radiation detection monitors.[4]

In fiscal year 2009, DOE transferred the Isotope Program from its Office of Nuclear Energy to its Office of Science and revised the program's mission to three purposes: (1) produce or distribute isotopes in short supply, their associated by-products and surplus materials, and deliver isotope-related services; (2) maintain the infrastructure required to produce and supply isotopes and related services; and (3) investigate and develop new or improved isotope production and processing techniques that can make new isotopes available for research and other applications. To meet this three-pronged mission, the Isotope Program operates from an annual budget consisting of yearly appropriations[5] and revenues from isotope sales. In fiscal year 2011, appropriations totaled almost $20 million, and revenues from sales of isotopes alone totaled almost $27 million, according to data provided by agency officials.

---

[3]GAO, *Managing Critical Isotopes: Weaknesses in DOE's Management of Helium-3 Delayed the Federal Response to a Critical Supply Shortage*, GAO-11-472 (Washington, D.C.: May 12, 2011).

[4]GAO, *Neutron Detectors: Alternatives to Using Helium-3*, GAO-11-753 (Washington, D.C.: Sept. 29, 2011).

[5]In this report, we use the phrase "yearly appropriations" to refer to funding that is received by DOE through the annual appropriations process, but has no restrictions on the time by which it must be obligated.

GAO-12-591 DOE's Isotope Program

In addition to DOE's Isotope Program, NNSA generates or provides some additional isotopes as by-products of the weapons program and research activities. Through its Office of Nuclear Materials Integration, NNSA makes these isotopes available to other federal entities, including DOE's Isotope Program, which then coordinates their sale and distribution to researchers and commercial entities.

Since 2008, the Isotope Program has been addressing programmatic risks and challenges as identified by external stakeholders as part of a series of program reviews. The risks and challenges the reviews identified included concerns over supply limitations for some isotopes, the need for long-term infrastructure investments to maintain the capacity for isotope production, and difficulties with accurately forecasting isotope demand. Specifically, in August 2008, DOE organized a workshop bringing together a wide range of stakeholders to discuss the nation's current and future isotope needs and to consider options for improving the availability of needed isotopes. This workshop identified 30 key isotopes that were in short supply at that time, including 12 whose supplies had been exhausted or were likely to run out within the following 3 years. Also in 2008, DOE requested that the Nuclear Science Advisory Committee form an isotope subcommittee to advise the program on specific isotope risks.[6] The subcommittee produced two reports in response: one identifying and setting priorities for compelling research opportunities using isotopes and another report presenting opportunities and priorities for ensuring a robust national isotope program. These reports highlighted short-term and long-term risks and challenges facing the Isotope Program, such as the program's reliance on DOE laboratories to produce certain isotopes. Specifically, the report expressed concern that the Isotope Program relies on the linear particle accelerators[7] at Brookhaven National Laboratory and Los Alamos National Laboratory for isotope production, even though isotope production is not the primary mission of these laboratories.

---

[6]The Nuclear Science Advisory Committee is an advisory committee that provides official advice to the Department of Energy and the National Science Foundation on basic nuclear science research. The lead responsibility for the direction of the advisory committee, selecting members, creating meeting agendas, and developing charges is shared by the two agencies.

[7]A particle accelerator uses electromagnetic forces to accelerate charged particles, such as electrons or protons. The resulting beam of fast-moving particles may be used for a variety of applications, including the creation of different isotopes.

In light of the importance of the isotopes sold by the Isotope Program and the various challenges it faces, you asked us to review the program. Specifically, our objectives were to determine (1) which isotopes are produced, sold, or distributed either by the Isotope Program or NNSA and how the two entities make isotopes available for commercial and research applications; (2) what steps the Isotope Program takes to provide isotopes for commercial and research applications; and (3) the extent to which DOE is assessing and mitigating risks facing the Isotope Program.

Scope and Methodology

To identify which isotopes are produced, sold, or distributed either by the Isotope Program or NNSA and how the two agencies make isotopes available for commercial and research applications, we reviewed the DOE Isotope Program's information on available isotopes, isotope sales data, and information on NNSA's isotopes. We also visited Oak Ridge National Laboratory in Tennessee, where the Isotope Program's business office and the program's inventory of stable isotopes are located, to view production facilities and interview officials about isotope production and sales. We interviewed officials at the national laboratories that produce isotopes for the Isotope Program: Brookhaven National Laboratory in New York, Idaho National Laboratory in Idaho, Los Alamos National Laboratory in New Mexico, Oak Ridge National Laboratory in Tennessee, and Pacific Northwest National Laboratory in Washington State. We also interviewed headquarters officials with the Isotope Program and NNSA about isotope production and how the two entities work together. To determine what steps the Isotope Program takes to provide isotopes for commercial and research applications, we reviewed the Isotope Program's production schedules, pricing policy, and documents related to how the program gathers information on customers' needs. We also interviewed representatives from commercial companies and researchers who purchase isotopes from the Isotope Program. We interviewed officials from the National Isotope Development Center; the Isotope Program; and Brookhaven, Los Alamos, and Oak Ridge National Laboratories because officials at these locations are involved in producing and selling isotopes to customers. To determine the extent to which DOE is assessing risks facing the Isotope Program, we reviewed reports from the Nuclear Science Advisory Committee's isotope subcommittee and the report from the isotope workshop DOE held in 2008. We also reviewed the strategic plans, risk assessment plans, and related documents from Brookhaven, Los Alamos, and Oak Ridge National Laboratories because the Isotope Program is the steward of isotope production at these sites. We reviewed and compared lists of high-priority isotopes that were prepared by the Isotope Program, the Nuclear Science Advisory

Committee's isotope subcommittee, the National Institutes of Health, and stakeholders at the 2008 isotope workshop. We also interviewed officials from the Isotope Program and Brookhaven, Los Alamos, and Oak Ridge National Laboratories to learn about risk assessment planning at each site and for the Isotope Program. In addition, we compared actions the Isotope Program is taking to assess risks with federal standards for internal control.[8]

We conducted this performance audit from June 2011 to May 2012, in accordance with generally accepted government auditing standards. Those standards require that we plan and perform the audit to obtain sufficient, appropriate evidence to provide a reasonable basis for our findings and conclusions based on our audit objectives. We believe that the evidence obtained provides a reasonable basis for our findings and conclusions based on our audit objectives.

Background

Isotope production and distribution have been part of DOE's mission since at least 1954, when the Atomic Energy Act of 1954 specified the role of the U.S. government in isotope distribution.[9] DOE's Isotope Program fills this role by providing isotopes to support the national and international need for a reliable supply for use in medicine, industry, and research. The Isotope Program provides both radioactive isotopes, called radioisotopes, and stable isotopes, which are not radioactive.[10] In addition, the Isotope Program provides a range of isotope-related services to customers worldwide. For example, the program may lease some stable isotopes and also provides irradiation and isotope-processing services for research and commercial applications.

DOE transferred the Isotope Program from the department's Office of Nuclear Energy to its Office of Science in 2009, at which time DOE restructured the program. The program currently consists of four DOE

---

[8]GAO, *Standards for Internal Control in the Federal Government*, GAO/AIMD-00-21.3.1 ("Green Book") (Washington, D.C.: November 1999).

[9]Atomic Energy Act of 1954, Pub. L. No. 83-703, 68 Stat. 919.

[10]Radioisotopes are radioactive—that is, they are unstable forms of elements that decay or disintegrate, emitting radiation. Some radioisotopes are found naturally, and others can be produced in nuclear reactors or particle accelerators. Stable isotopes do not decay or emit radiation and are therefore not radioactive.

headquarters employees who oversee operations and set policy, plus the National Isotope Development Center, which is a virtual organization consisting of DOE contract employees located at Los Alamos National Laboratory and Oak Ridge National Laboratory. National Isotope Development Center employees carry out day-to-day operations of the Isotope Program, which include interacting with the isotope user community though a variety of outreach activities, monitoring short-term and long-term isotope demand, coordinating isotope production across DOE's isotope production facilities, and distributing isotopes. The National Isotope Development Center includes DOE contract employees at the Isotope Business Office, located at Oak Ridge National Laboratory, who manage business operations involved in the production, sale, and distribution of isotopes. In addition, officials from the National Isotope Development Center and DOE headquarters coordinate with many federal programs, including the National Institutes of Health, to identify current and future isotope needs.

The Isotope Program produces most of its radioisotopes at three DOE production sites: the linear particle accelerators at Brookhaven National Laboratory in New York and Los Alamos National Laboratory in New Mexico, and the nuclear reactor at Oak Ridge National Laboratory in Tennessee. The program also produces a small number of radioisotopes at the Pacific Northwest National Laboratory in Washington State and at Idaho National Laboratory. The DOE facilities associated with the Isotope Program are recognized as uniquely capable of producing radioisotopes. Although the Isotope Program uses these DOE sites to produce radioisotopes, the program does not manage all the sites' operations. Rather, the Isotope Program shares the use of these sites with other missions, which consist of a diverse combination of DOE activities related to nuclear science, materials research, or defense. The production sites are therefore not always available to the Isotope Program, and at times the program may not control the timing and duration of isotope production.

The Isotope Program relies on appropriations and revenues from isotope sales for funding its operations. Both yearly appropriations and sales revenues are deposited into a revolving fund[11] from which the program draws funds to operate its facilities, produce isotopes, pay employees' salaries, and fund research, among other activities. Funds remain available to the program in the revolving fund, which allows the program to carry over balances from year to year, giving the program budgeting flexibility. Table 1 shows the Isotope Program's revolving fund balances, annual appropriations, annual sales revenues, and obligations to operate the program for fiscal years 2009 through 2011. The Isotope Program's annual spending on research and development is generally aimed at developing new or more efficient isotope production techniques.

Table 1: Revenues and Obligations of DOE's Isotope Program, Fiscal Years 2009 through 2011

	Fiscal year 2009	Fiscal year 2010	Fiscal year 2011
Revenues			
Carryover from previous fiscal year	$14,341,000	$24,235,000	$16,844,000
Sales revenues and other resources[a]	$25,373,000	$18,620,000	$28,837,000
Appropriations	$24,760,000	$19,116,000	$19,670,000
American Recovery and Reinvestment Act funds[b]	$14,617,000	$0.00	$0.00
Total funding	**$79,092,000**	**$61,971,000**	**$65,351,000**
Obligations			
Research and development	$5,424,000	$6,151,000	$1,644,000
Operations	$49,433,000	$38,976,000	$45,696,000
Total obligations	**$54,857,000**	**$45,127,000**	**$47,360,000**
Carryover to next fiscal year	$24,235,000	$16,844,000	$17,991,000

Source: DOE.

Note: Numbers may not sum because of rounding.

[a]Sales revenues and other resources include revenues received for isotope sales and isotope-related services, as well as funds received from federal and other entities.

[b]The Isotope Program received funds from the American Recovery and Reinvestment Act in fiscal year 2009.

---

[11]The Isotope Program's revolving fund was first established under Public Law 101-101, Title III. Both yearly appropriations and revenues from the sales of isotopes are deposited into the revolving fund, which the program then draws from to fund its operations. Any funds remaining in the revolving fund at the end of a fiscal year are carried over to the next fiscal year.

The Isotope Program sold isotopes or provided isotope-related services to more than 100 customers in fiscal year 2011, both in the United States and internationally, with 6 of those customers accounting for more than 80 percent of all sales revenue in fiscal year 2011. More than 95 percent of the Isotope Program's annual revenue came from the sale of eight different isotopes in fiscal year 2011; these eight isotopes generated almost $26 million in revenue (see table 2).

Table 2: The Eight Top-Selling Isotopes of DOE's Isotope Program in Fiscal Year 2011

Isotope	2011 revenue
Strontium-82	$11,560,000
Californium-252	$7,657,000[a]
Helium-3	$3,255,000
Germanium-68	$1,910,000
Nickel-63	$576,000
Strontium-90	$297,000
Actinium-225	$263,000
Lithium-6	$223,000
Total	$25,741,000

Source: DOE.

[a]This amount includes $2 million that was paid in fiscal year 2009 by customers as advance payments for future production costs.

DOE's Isotope Program and NNSA Together Produce or Make Available over 300 Isotopes for Research and Commercial Applications

DOE's Isotope Program produces or makes available for sale and distribution over 300 different isotopes for research and commercial applications. NNSA generates or provides additional isotopes that are transferred to other federal agencies or sold by the Isotope Program (see app. I). The program may produce or make available to customers more than 300 different isotopes, but fewer than that number are sold in a given year. In fiscal year 2011, for example, the program sold less than 170 distinct isotopes. The isotopes sold by the Isotope Program can be categorized as (1) radioisotopes currently produced by the Isotope Program at DOE production sites;[12] (2) stable isotopes from the Isotope Program's inventory, which are no longer produced in the United States; and (3) isotopes generated or provided by NNSA as by-products of its nuclear weapons program (see table 3).[13]

Table 3: Isotopes Available for Sale by DOE's Isotope Program

Category	Number available
Radioisotopes produced by the Isotope Program	55
Stable isotopes in the Isotope Program's inventory	243
Radioisotopes generated or provided by NNSA	10

Source: DOE.

The Isotope Program is responsible for the production and sale of 55 radioisotopes produced at five DOE laboratories—Brookhaven, Los Alamos, Oak Ridge, Pacific Northwest, and Idaho National Laboratories. In any given year, the Isotope Program does not produce all 55 radioisotopes; rather, it produces and sells those for which customer demand exists and is unmet by supply from commercial sources. At times, the Isotope Program may choose to begin or stop producing a given isotope depending on whether commercial entities are meeting demand, whether an isotope's market price is so high that it inhibits research, or whether DOE has the facilities necessary to produce the isotope, among other considerations. For example, in 2009 the Isotope Program reestablished production of californium-252, which is used in a

---

[12]Some isotopes that are produced by DOE's Isotope Program are extracted from other materials held in inventory. For example, americium-241 is extracted from other materials.

[13]In addition to these categories, many radioisotopes that are not produced or sold by DOE's Isotope Program are available from commercial entities, which produce and sell isotopes on the open market.

variety of applications, including oil exploration and medical applications, because of customer demand. Californium-252 was previously produced by the Isotope Program in partnership with NNSA and sold through the Isotope Program. When NNSA no longer needed californium-252 for its mission, it stopped supporting its production in 2007, according to an Isotope Program official. The Isotope Program worked with a coalition of commercial customers to continue producing californium-252 to meet the needs of the coalition and researchers. Isotope Program officials indicated, however, that a change like this in the program's production portfolio does not happen often.

In addition to the radioisotopes it produces, the Isotope Program also maintains an inventory of 243 stable isotopes that it sells to customers. These stable isotopes were produced by DOE until the late 1990s at DOE facilities that are no longer in use, and since these isotopes are stable, they can remain in storage almost indefinitely. Because stable isotopes are no longer produced, supplies of some of them have been exhausted, and supplies of others are dwindling. Specifically, according to current Isotope Program data, nine stable isotopes that were in the program's inventory are no longer available, and six have less than 10 years' supply at current rates of use (see table 4).

Table 4: Stable Isotopes Sold by DOE's Isotope Program with a Supply of Less Than 10 Years

Isotope	Supply (in years)
Gadolinium-157	0.5
Nickel-62	4.5
Neodymium-150	4.8
Gallium-69	5.9
Tungsten-183	7.6
Tungsten-182	9.9

Source: DOE.

According to program officials, the Isotope Program occasionally purchases quantities of some stable isotopes from foreign sources, such as Russia, in an effort to maintain the program's supply. Isotope Program officials explained that the program buys stable isotopes from foreign sources and then resells them to domestic customers because the Isotope Program can take steps to ensure isotope quality and offer other services that foreign suppliers are unwilling to provide, such as leasing some stable isotopes for research or other applications. Given dwindling supplies in DOE's inventory and increasing reliance on foreign sources, whose supplies for some isotopes are also dwindling, the Nuclear Science Advisory Committee recommended in 2009 that the Isotope Program reestablish capability to produce stable isotopes in the United States. The Isotope Program is funding several projects in response to this recommendation, including the development of stable isotope production at Oak Ridge National Laboratory, in part, using funds it received in fiscal year 2009 from the American Recovery and Reinvestment Act. Isotope Program officials stated that the project is expected to be completed in 2014.

The Isotope Program sells an additional 10 isotopes that are provided by NNSA. The program does not control the supply of these isotopes but coordinates with NNSA to sell and distribute them. Isotope Program officials coordinate with NNSA's Office of Nuclear Materials Integration, which was created in 2008 to work across DOE to, among other things, make NNSA's isotopes and other materials available to government entities. For example, NNSA has a stockpile of lithium-6, some of which it provides to the Isotope Program to sell; lithium-6 is used in research and security equipment to detect neutrons given off by other nuclear materials. The Isotope Program also coordinates with NNSA to produce isotopes that the Isotope Program does not have the capability to produce, such as americium-241, which is used in smoke detectors and medical diagnostic devices.

In Providing Commercial Isotopes, DOE's Isotope Program May Be Forgoing Revenue That Could Further Support Its Mission

To provide isotopes for commercial and research applications, the Isotope Program takes steps to determine the demand for isotopes, coordinate production across production sites, and set prices for isotopes, but the program is not using thorough assessments to establish prices for commercial isotopes. The Isotope Program has flexibility to set prices at market levels for isotopes sold for commercial applications but instead, for most isotopes where the program is the only domestic supplier, sets prices at the level necessary to recover its cost to produce them. In setting prices for commercial isotopes, however, the Isotope Program is not assessing the value of the isotope to the customer or prices of alternatives, as permitted under its pricing policy. As a result, the Isotope Program may be forgoing revenue that could be used to further its mission and address unmet needs.

To Ensure the Availability of Isotopes, DOE's Isotope Program Determines Demand, Coordinates Production, and Sets Prices

To ensure the availability of isotopes for research and commercial applications, the Isotope Program annually determines demand, coordinates production across its production sites, and sets prices for selling isotopes. To determine annual demand, Isotope Program officials said they start with a general sense of demand based on historical sales data and frequent interaction with customers, through which they learn about changes in isotope needs. According to program officials, the Isotope Program asks customers to provide information on expected demand for the next year and as far as 5 years into the future, although some customers said such estimates are difficult to make. The Isotope Program also takes customers' orders for isotopes throughout the year via e-mail, telephone, or the program's website. These orders, for radioisotopes and stable isotopes, are received by the Isotope Program's business office. To determine annual demand for strontium-82, for example, Isotope Program officials ask customers how much strontium-82 they need for the coming year, and each customer commits to a certain amount for that year. These customers then provide updates throughout the year to clarify actual strontium-82 quantities and delivery dates.

Orders for stable isotopes are received and processed throughout the year by the Isotope Program, but producing radioisotopes to meet demand requires considerable planning, according to program officials. When the Isotope Program receives an order for a stable isotope, such as calcium-48, it can be filled from the existing inventory of stable isotopes. In contrast, orders for radioisotopes are taken throughout the year and used to plan production during the Isotope Program's annual production planning meeting. The outcome of the meeting is a production schedule for the production sites, which identifies radioisotopes needed for the coming year. The production schedule outlines the projected dates when each isotope will be produced and which site will produce it, but the exact schedule depends on a variety of factors. Specifically, because the Isotope Program generally does not control the operation of reactors or accelerators, it uses the facilities at the same time as other DOE programs, thus limiting the Isotope Program's capability to produce isotopes, according to program officials. For instance, according to program officials, the accelerator at Los Alamos National Laboratory typically operates from July through December, and the accelerator at Brookhaven National Laboratory typically operates from January through June. In addition, because many radioisotopes decay rapidly after production, they need to be delivered in a timely manner, and officials must consider customers' desired delivery times when determining the production schedule. For instance, strontium-82 has a half-life[14] of about 26 days and, according to one customer, must arrive predictably to be used for its intended purpose. Other isotopes have even shorter life spans and need to be delivered on a precise day before they decay too much to be useful. An Isotope Program official told us that that the production schedule is adjusted throughout the year as customers' demands change, as new isotopes are ordered, as facilities experience unanticipated shutdowns, or for other reasons. During our discussions with several Isotope Program customers, we found that they were generally satisfied with the timeliness of isotope delivery.

To set prices for radioisotopes, program officials annually request detailed production cost data, including both direct and indirect costs, from the individual DOE and NNSA production sites that provided the isotope. According to program officials, direct costs include labor costs and costs for chemical processing, among others; indirect costs include facility maintenance costs and other infrastructure costs. These officials said that the Isotope Program uses cost data from the production sites to determine the sales price for each isotope and prices isotopes differently depending on whether the intended use is for research or commercial applications. For research applications, isotope prices are set to recover only direct costs. In addition, according to program officials, research isotopes are priced by unit, instead of batch, so researchers can buy small quantities of isotopes and not have to pay for production of an entire batch.[15] Thus, prices for research isotopes are subsidized by the Isotope Program, with indirect costs covered by the program's yearly appropriation. Program officials told us that the intent of this subsidy is to promote independent research on uses of isotopes by making them more affordable to the research community. Overall, the result is that some research isotopes are priced significantly lower—from about 9 percent to 75 percent less, in some cases—than the same isotope used for commercial applications.

---

[14]The half-life of a radioactive isotope is the time required for half the unstable atoms to disintegrate, or decay, and release their radiation.

[15]A batch of isotopes is the amount produced by an entire production cycle. Researchers may require a smaller quantity of an isotope than what is produced in a batch.

For isotopes used in commercial applications, prices are generally set to recover, at a minimum, the full cost of isotope production, including both direct costs and indirect costs. For orders of large quantities of commercial isotopes, the per-unit cost of production is lower, so the Isotope Program can provide volume discounts. In addition, according to program officials, the Isotope Program adds a nominal fee to isotopes sold commercially, which amounts to approximately 10 percent in additional costs for commercial isotopes—6 percent for administrative costs to process orders for isotopes and 4 percent as a contingency charge to cover unanticipated events. A recent unanticipated event, for example, occurred in fiscal year 2011. According to a program official, orders for strontium-82, which had accounted for more than a third of the program's sales revenue in 2010, decreased significantly and unexpectedly as the result of a recall of the cardiac imaging device that was the main application for strontium-82. According to program officials, the Isotope Program sales revenue declined by over $5 million from July 2011 through January 2012 as a result, and program officials said they had to draw from the revolving fund to maintain operations.

For stable isotopes that are sold from its existing inventory, Isotope Program officials told us that prices are based on historical production costs adjusted annually for inflation, rather than on current replacement costs; the prices are the same regardless of whether they are used for research or commercial applications. Officials told us that they do not base the prices of stable isotopes on current replacement costs because DOE does not have the capability to produce these stable isotopes. Isotope Program officials told us that market studies were in the early stages of being carried out in preparation for reestablishing the capability to produce stable isotopes in 2014; these studies are intended to help the program determine which stable isotopes to produce and in what quantities.

In Setting Prices for Most Commercial Isotopes, DOE's Isotope Program May Be Forgoing Revenue That Could Further Support Its Mission

The Isotope Program generally charges full cost recovery for commercial isotopes, but the program has not fully assessed the pricing of most of the commercial isotopes it sells, as required by its current policy, such as assessing the value of the isotopes to the customer or prices of similar isotopes. As a result, the program may be discouraging others from producing isotopes and, at the same time, forgoing sales revenue that could further support its mission to deliver needed isotopes, maintain isotope production infrastructure, and support research, in addition to addressing unmet needs. The Atomic Energy Act of 1954 states that the federal government should be reasonably compensated for isotopes it sells and that isotope prices should not discourage commercial isotope producers from entering the market. Aside from these constraints, the Isotope Program has broad authority in setting isotope prices. To this end, the Isotope Program established a pricing policy in 1990 that provides latitude for establishing prices at full cost recovery or at market prices that are higher or lower than full cost recovery, but also states that when a market price already exists that is higher than full cost recovery, the market price should be used. The policy also states that prices should be assessed annually and that additional factors may be considered when establishing prices, including the number of suppliers, demand, competitors' prices, and the value of the isotope to the customer. This policy appears to be consistent with guidance from the Office of Management and Budget on the sale of government goods and services, which suggests that sales should be self-sustaining and based on market prices.[16] In cases where no market currently exists, such as many of the commercial isotopes produced and sold by the Isotope Program, the Office of Management and Budget's guidance states that prices can be set by taking into account the prevailing prices for goods that are the same as or substantially similar to those provided by the government and then adjusting the supply made available, prices of the goods, or both so that there will be neither a shortage nor a surplus.

In practice, according to program officials, the Isotope Program generally sets the prices for commercial isotopes at full cost recovery—the lowest price possible for the program to recover its costs for providing an isotope. According to Isotope Program officials, prices for commercial isotopes are set above full cost recovery only when a higher price for the isotope already exists in the commercial market and pricing the isotope at full cost recovery would be low enough to distort the existing market.[17] If isotope prices are artificially low, the Isotope Program's price may, in turn, discourage private entities from entering the isotope market, discourage commercial entities or researchers from exploring alternatives to using some isotopes, or encourage overconsumption. Isotope Program officials offered two reasons why the program charges no more than full cost

[16]Office of Management and Budget, Circular A-25.

[17]According to program officials, at present the Isotope Program has set the price above full cost recovery for helium-3 and two other isotopes. These three isotopes are priced above full cost recovery because, according to officials, market prices exist that are greater than the full cost of production, and setting the prices lower would distort their market prices.

recovery for most of the commercial isotopes it sells. First, officials told us they believe many customers are sensitive to prices and already consider prices for isotopes to be too high. Isotope Program officials said that some potential customers are already unwilling or unable to pay current prices for many isotopes and that some existing customers have suggested that any price increases would make isotopes unaffordable and force them to seek other isotope sources. Second, Isotope Program officials stated that the program's role is not to maximize revenue from isotope sales but to make isotopes widely available. Isotope Program officials told us that, consistent with the program's mission and the Atomic Energy Act, the Isotope Program strives to supply isotopes at reasonable prices to encourage their use.

For most of the isotopes it produces and sells, however, program officials told us that in instances where the Isotope Program is the only domestic supplier, the program has not formally determined the value of isotopes to commercial customers or prices of alternatives. Program officials told us that they gain a sense of customers' value for isotopes through various interactions with these customers, although they did not provide a formal analysis as described in the pricing policy. According to documents provided by the Isotope Program, the program has also collected limited market information for a small number of isotopes, but these studies are outdated or do not consider pricing. For example, a market study provided by the Isotope Program that was conducted in 2002 projects the future demand and potential revenues for 25 different radioisotopes used in medicine over the next 5 to 10 years, but that study is now outdated. Additionally, according to one program official, the market study to be conducted for the Isotope Program's isotopes beginning in 2012 is to provide information on which isotopes are in greatest demand so officials will know which stable isotopes to produce, although the study will not address isotope prices.

Without formally assessing the value of isotopes to commercial customers or the prices of alternatives for isotopes where the Isotope Program is the only domestic supplier, the Isotope Program does not know if its full cost recovery prices for isotopes are in fact discouraging others from producing isotopes, discouraging commercial entities and researchers from developing alternatives, and/or encouraging overconsumption. If assessments of customers' value for isotopes and the prices of potential alternatives show that prices can be increased above full cost recovery for some commercial isotopes, the additional revenue could be used to further the Isotope Program's mission and address unmet needs. For example, revenues could be used to fund research for the development of new or more efficient production capabilities for additional isotopes. Also, the Nuclear Science Advisory Committee recommended in its report on opportunities and priorities for ensuring a robust national isotope program that the Isotope Program invest in a facility dedicated to producing radioisotopes. Such a facility, according to the advisory committee, is the most cost-effective option to position the Isotope Program to ensure continuous access to many of the needed radioactive isotopes. Program officials told us they were developing a new pricing policy, but because the policy is in draft form and subject to change, we were unable to determine, among other things, whether the new policy would provide direction on how commercial isotope prices are to reflect the value of the isotope to the customer, the prices of alternatives, or both.

DOE's Isotope Program Has Taken Some Actions to Identify and Manage Risks, but Its Efforts Are Not Comprehensive

The Isotope Program has begun taking some actions to identify and mitigate risks to achieving its mission of producing isotopes, such as the risk of relying on sales of a small number of commercial isotopes for a large percentage of its revenues, but without first establishing clear, consistent program objectives, the program's risk assessment efforts are not comprehensive.

DOE's Isotope Program Is Taking Varied Actions to Identify and Mitigate Program Risks

The Isotope Program is taking some actions to assess risks to achieving its mission, including identifying high-priority isotopes and using its revolving fund to mitigate risks from unforeseen events. Risk assessment first involves, according to federal standards for internal control,[18] identifying and analyzing risks associated with achieving a program's objectives and then determining how to manage such risks. Our analysis shows that the Isotope Program currently assesses risks through several methods. First, Isotope Program officials, National Isotope Development Center staff, and production site managers identify risks to providing isotopes by monitoring long-term changes in demand within the isotope community that could affect isotope supply. Unlike determining demand

---

[18]GAO/AIMD-00-21.3.1.

for annual production planning, these monitoring activities focus on changes that could influence isotope supply and demand in the longer term, such as new products that could eventually increase demand for a specific isotope, according to Isotope Program documents. According to program officials, long-term monitoring activities help them stay abreast of changes in the isotope community that may warrant adjustments to the program's product portfolio. In addition, program officials told us that these activities play a role in long-range program planning, as well as informing decisions regarding research and development. Some monitoring activities are performed on a continuous basis, such as discussing new developments in isotope uses and production capacity with foreign isotope suppliers, while others occur once or a few times a year, such as attending industry conferences to collect information about new commercial products that use isotopes. To manage risks created by changes in demand, according to Isotope Program officials, the program gathers additional information on the issue and may convene workgroups that bring together isotope community stakeholders to discuss trends for one or several isotopes. For example, the program organized a working group in 2008 with representatives from the National Institutes of Health to explore supply and demand for medical research isotopes. It also convened a workshop of federal stakeholders in January 2012 to discuss isotope priorities, supply, and demand among federal entities.

The Isotope Program also assesses risks to the program by identifying high-priority isotopes—those at risk of supply problems, either because the isotopes are already in short supply or are important to users. Five lists of high-priority isotopes have been created by isotope stakeholders, and Isotope Program officials said that they use the lists to set program priorities. The following describes each of the lists and the entity that created them:

- The 2008 workshop of isotope community stakeholders created an unranked list of more than 47 isotopes considered to be in short supply or unavailable from DOE for research and applications.

- In 2009, the National Institutes of Health isotope working group developed a list of important medical research isotopes that are not commercially available; the list was updated and ranked in order of priority in January 2012.

- In 2009, the Nuclear Science Advisory Committee's isotope subcommittee produced a list of isotopes important for medical and scientific research purposes and prioritized them according to the importance of the research opportunities.

- In 2011, the National Isotope Development Center listed stable isotopes in priority order according to the importance of the isotopes in research and commercial applications.

- In 2011, the National Isotope Development Center listed specific isotopes called nuclear materials and heavy elements and prioritized them on the basis of importance of the isotopes in research and commercial applications.

Program officials told us they use the high-priority lists to establish program priorities, such as determining what research and development initiatives to undertake. For example, according to program officials, for some of the listed isotopes, the program has reached out to universities to research new production methods. In addition, the Nuclear Science Advisory Committee's isotope subcommittee's list serves as a criterion for awarding research and development grants; research projects for isotopes on the list receive higher priority for funding than projects for isotopes not on this list. Four of the lists rank the isotopes in order of priority, and one does not; the prioritized lists rank isotopes according to different criteria. For example, the National Institutes of Health prioritized isotopes on the basis of their importance to medical research, while the National Isotope Development Center prioritized isotopes on the basis of their importance to research and commercial applications. In total, 104 different isotopes appear on the five lists—about 18 percent of the total number of isotopes currently available from the program. Although a few isotopes are found on more than one list, most isotopes are found on only a single list.

The Isotope Program mitigates risks by using the flexibility of its revolving fund to help manage unexpected events, such as losses in revenues. The Isotope Program is authorized to carry over revenues and yearly appropriations in its revolving fund from fiscal year to fiscal year. The law authorizing the revolving fund provides the program broad discretion for managing the fund, stating that appropriations and revenues deposited into the fund are to be used for "activities related to the production, distribution, and sale of isotopes and related services."[19] The program uses its flexibility in managing the revolving fund to prepare for and mitigate unexpected events. To this end, of the 10 percent fee the program adds to the price of isotopes sold to commercial customers, it deposits 4 percent into the revolving fund to cover unanticipated events. For example, the program drew on the fund to maintain operations in 2011 and 2012 in the face of a significant, unexpected decline in revenue from the sale of strontium-82.

The Isotope Program also assesses risks at its three primary isotope production facilities by identifying and managing risks to the production sites. The isotope production facilities at Oak Ridge and Los Alamos National Laboratories in 2011 developed plans that describe processes for identifying and managing risks at the sites that could be detrimental to isotope production.[20] The plans lay out which production site elements—such as infrastructure, chemical processing, and shipping processes—should be assessed for risks and describe how site officials are to determine the likelihood and consequence of any identified risks. In conjunction with the plans, Oak Ridge and Los Alamos National Laboratories created spreadsheets for tracking risks—called risk registers—that list each identified risk, its likelihood, consequence, and mitigation strategy, among other things. Many of the identified risks focus on equipment failure or malfunction, such as risks that components of a processing facility shut down unexpectedly. Other risks are related to management and regulatory issues. Brookhaven National Laboratory has developed a similar risk-tracking spreadsheet that focuses exclusively on risks to production equipment. According to one program official, the risk management plans and spreadsheets help the program set priorities for investments that will help manage risks. For example, on the basis of Los Alamos National Laboratory's risk register, the program decided to modify its facilities to reduce radiation risks. These risk management plans and risk registers are specific to the three production sites and do not identify risks to the entire Isotope Program.

---

[19]Energy and Water Development Appropriations Act, 1990 (Pub. L. No. 101-101, 103 Stat. 641).

[20]The plans also describe a similar process for identifying and managing opportunities. The third production site at Brookhaven National Laboratory has not developed a similar risk and opportunity assessment and management plan.

DOE's Isotope Program Does Not Have Clear Objectives That Enable It to Comprehensively Assess Program Risks

The Isotope Program is taking risk assessment actions without first establishing clear, consistent objectives; that is, it does not identify and mitigate risks to achieving program objectives in a comprehensive way. One of the federal standards for internal control—risk assessment—states that a precondition to risk assessment is the establishment of clear, consistent objectives. Long-term goals and objectives describe how the program will implement its mission, when actions will be taken, and what resources are needed to reach these goals. Once objectives have been set, the program then identifies risks that could keep it from efficiently and effectively achieving those objectives at all levels. After risks have been identified, they are to be analyzed for their possible effect and decisions made on how to manage the identified risks.[21]

DOE's Isotope Program has not established clear, consistent objectives to serve as a basis for risk assessment. Isotope Program officials told us the program is relying on two reports from the Nuclear Science Advisory Committee's isotope subcommittee to guide its decisions and that these two reports provide adequate guidance. Together, these reports recommend 15 different long-term actions for the program but do not provide clear objectives for the program or a description of how those objectives are to be achieved. For example, one report recommends that the program construct and operate an electromagnetic isotope separator facility for stable and long-lived radioisotopes but does not describe how this recommendation is to be achieved. The report also does not provide criteria for measuring progress toward meeting this or other recommendations. Isotope Program officials told us, however, that the program is undertaking a new strategic planning process in 2012 to develop a 5-year strategic plan.

Without clearly defined objectives that lay out what the program is to accomplish, the Isotope Program cannot be assured that its current risk assessment and mitigation efforts focus on the most significant issues that could impede achievement of its mission. For example, the program does not have objectives that could provide direction about which of the five high-priority isotope lists warrants the most attention. Instead, program officials reported that they take all the lists into account when making production and research decisions. They could not tell us if one list of isotopes is a higher priority than the others. Furthermore, without

---

[21]GAO/AIMD-00-21.3.1.

clear objectives, program officials cannot determine how important one isotope on a list is relative to isotopes on the other lists because they are prioritized using different criteria, or they are not prioritized. For example,

- thallium-203 is ranked as the most important isotope on the National Isotope Development Center's list of stable isotopes;

- actinium-225, astatine-211, and lead-212 are identified as the most important isotopes in medicine, pharmaceuticals, and biology in the report of the Nuclear Science Advisory Committee's isotope subcommittee; and

- californium-252 and radium-225 are identified as the most important isotopes for physical science and engineering in this same report.

Without consolidating the multiple lists of high-priority isotopes, however, it is unclear which isotopes have greater priority than others. Thus, program managers may not be focusing limited resources on the most important isotopes.

Furthermore, because the program does not have clear objectives, it cannot be assured that it is assessing and mitigating risks from all relevant external and internal sources. In particular, the program has not assessed risks associated with relying on a small handful of isotopes for a large percentage of annual revenue. This issue is important in the context of the unexpected decline in strontium-82 orders that occurred in 2011, which resulted in a large reduction in expected revenue. The program likely could not have anticipated this loss, but comprehensive risk assessment efforts might have identified the risk of relying on strontium-82 and a few other isotopes for a large amount of revenue. Without identifying all relevant risks, the program also cannot determine how to manage such risks. When the strontium-82 orders declined, the program was able to rely on its revolving fund to make up for unexpected revenue loss, but it may not always be able to do so. Isotope Program officials told us there is no guiding document for how the revolving fund should be spent or managed. Without guidance on how to manage the revolving fund in a way that helps mitigate risk, the program cannot be assured that it will be able to continue using the fund to both advance program missions and mitigate risks. For example, if the program unexpectedly loses revenue for several years in a row, the revolving fund may not provide sufficient reserves to maintain program operations.

Conclusions

Managing the production and sale of over 300 different isotopes for various research, commercial, industrial, and medical applications is a daunting task. With a wide variety of customers, whose needs may change over time, it is difficult for the Isotope Program to determine demand, plan production, and project revenue streams to avoid shortages of important isotopes or interruptions in the revenues that help to sustain the program. The Isotope Program is taking several actions to assess demand and plan production. In addition, the Isotope Program has clearly defined under what circumstances it will charge reduced prices for research isotopes. The program has not, however, defined what factors it will consider when it sets prices for isotopes sold commercially, including defining under what circumstances it will set prices for such isotopes at or above full cost recovery. Without transparency in decisions on pricing, it is unclear if Isotope Program officials are setting prices consistently. Moreover, in the absence of established market prices and without current information on the value customers place on isotopes and prices of similar products, the Isotope Program cannot ensure that the prices it sets are appropriate and thus may be forgoing revenues that could be used to further its mission and ensure the program's long-term viability.

As the Isotope Program moves forward with its process to establish a 5-year strategic plan, creating clear goals and objectives is the first step in being able to identify and manage risks to achieving the program's mission. Identifying high-priority isotopes that may need additional oversight is a good step toward managing risks, but without consolidating those lists and prioritizing them, program managers may not direct limited resources toward the most important isotopes.

Finally, when the Isotope Program's revenues from strontium-82 unexpectedly stopped, program officials were fortunate to have the revolving fund to mitigate the unexpected loss in revenue and maintain operations without disrupting supplies of other isotopes. Without clear guidance on when and how to use the revolving fund to mitigate future unexpected losses in revenue, the program cannot ensure that it will have sufficient funds to maintain operations, or for other activities, such as funding research and other projects that help the Isotope Program achieve its mission.

Recommendations for Executive Action

We are making four recommendations to the Secretary of Energy designed to improve the Isotope Program's transparency in setting prices and efficiency in managing isotopes. Specifically, we recommend that the Secretary of Energy direct the Isotope Program to take the following four actions:

- Clearly define the factors to be considered when the program sets prices for isotopes sold commercially, including defining under what circumstances it will set prices at or above full cost recovery. This should include assessing, when appropriate, current information on the value of isotopes to customers and the prices of similar products.

- In conjunction with strategic planning efforts already under way, create clear goals and objectives to serve as a basis for risk assessment, identify risks to achieving its goals and objectives, and determine what actions to take to manage the risks.

- Consolidate the lists of high-priority isotopes so the program can ensure that its resources are focused on the most important isotopes.

- Establish clear guidance for managing the revolving fund to ensure that the fund is sufficient to use as a contingency for unexpected losses in revenue.

Agency Comments and Our Evaluation

We provided a draft of this report to DOE for review and comment. In its written response, reproduced in appendix II, DOE explained that our recommendations will generally be addressed through the Isotope Program's current efforts to update its pricing policy and develop a strategic plan. DOE took exception, however, to our characterization of how the Isotope Program sets prices for commercial isotopes. Specifically, according to DOE's letter, the Isotope Program does consider "value of isotopes to customers" when setting prices for commercial isotopes. Nevertheless, none of the documents provided by the Isotope Program during our review show that the program conducted a current, formal analysis of what customers are willing to pay for commercial isotopes. Our report points out that program officials gain a sense of the value customers place on commercial isotopes through informal interactions with the customers themselves. Such interactions, in our view, do not provide a rigorous approach to determining a customer's value for commercial isotopes as customers generally strive to obtain needed materials, including isotopes, at the lowest possible cost. We are encouraged to see that, according to DOE's comments, the Isotope

Program's updated pricing policy is to identify which factors are to be considered in setting prices, including formal analysis of the value of commercial isotopes to customers.

In its comments, DOE expressed concern that our report suggests maximizing revenue and pricing commercial isotopes to increase revenue. DOE explained that the Isotope Program generally sets prices to fulfill the mandate established by the Atomic Energy Act of 1954 to provide isotopes at prices that do not discourage their use. Our report does not emphasize maximizing revenue or setting prices solely to increase revenue. It does point out that the Isotope Program has not performed the formal market analyses required by its own pricing policy. DOE further stated that the Isotope Program considers several factors when determining prices for commercial isotopes, including a "bottom-up activity-based costing for isotope production," and it has initiated two market studies that will provide input into the assessment of market prices. Comprehensive market studies would determine the prices customers are willing to pay for isotopes and prices of alternatives, among other factors, and would thus determine if the Isotope Program's prices for commercial isotopes are set at the appropriate level. Such analyses would also show whether the full-cost-recovery price, which is used for all but three of the commercially sold isotopes, is resulting in unintended, but avoidable, consequences. General economic considerations suggest that setting prices of isotopes at artificially low levels could have unintended consequences such as discouraging other entities from producing isotopes, discouraging commercial entities and researchers from developing alternatives, and encouraging overconsumption. Furthermore, our report points out that the Atomic Energy Act of 1954 states that isotope prices should not discourage commercial isotope producers from entering the market.

With regard to our recommendations, DOE's letter indicates that three of our four recommendations are being addressed through the Isotope Program's present efforts to update its pricing policy and develop a comprehensive strategic plan and risk assessment. With regard to our fourth recommendation—to consolidate and prioritize isotopes from the lists of high-priority isotopes—DOE stated that it "will need to assess the value added of doing an overall prioritization." DOE further states that even though an isotope may be a high priority for the isotope community, there is no guarantee that an entity is capable of producing it. In our view, this situation highlights the need for our recommendation. The Isotope Program has done outreach with the isotope community to identify the most important isotopes and has created a peer-review process that considers isotopes on the various high-priority lists as one of its factors in selecting projects for funding. This process alone, however, cannot ensure that the program's resources are accurately focused on the most-needed isotopes. Therefore, we believe it is up to the Isotope Program to consolidate the lists of high-priority isotopes and develop criteria to determine on which isotopes resources are to be focused.

Finally, DOE's letter stated that we mischaracterized NNSA's mission, which does not include providing isotopes to stakeholders. We clarified this statement and have made changes throughout the report as needed. DOE also provided technical comments that we incorporated in the report as appropriate.

As agreed with your offices, unless you publicly announce the contents of this report earlier, we plan no further distribution until 30 days from the report date. At that time, we will send copies to the appropriate congressional committees, Secretary of Energy, and other interested parties. In addition, the report will be available at no charge on the GAO website at http://www.gao.gov.

If you or your staff members have any questions about this report, please contact me at (202) 512-3841 or aloisee@gao.gov. Contact points for our Offices of Congressional Relations and Public Affairs may be found on the last page of this report. GAO staff who made key contributions to this report are listed in appendix III.

Gene Aloise
Director
Natural Resources and Environment

Appendix I: Isotopes Available from DOE's Isotope Program

This table identifies the isotopes provided at the time of this report for sale by the Department of Energy's (DOE) Isotope Development and Production for Research and Applications program (Isotope Program). According to Isotope Program officials, the availability of these isotopes may change and some isotopes may be provided in different chemical forms. For example, bromine-79 is available as sodium bromide but also as potassium bromide, silver bromide, and ammonium bromide. The table also shows how the Isotope Program classifies each isotope—as a radioisotope or stable isotope—and if an isotope is provided by the National Nuclear Security Administration (NNSA) and sold by the Isotope Program.

Isotope	Radioisotope	Stable isotope	Provided by NNSA
Actinium-225	X		
Americium-243	X		X
Antimony-121		X	
Antimony-123		X	
Argon-36		X	
Argon-40		X	
Arsenic-72	X		
Arsenic-73	X		
Barium-130		X	
Barium-132		X	
Barium-134		X	
Barium-135		X	
Barium-136		X	
Barium-137		X	
Barium-138		X	
Berkelium-249	X		
Beryllium-7	X		
Bismuth-207	X		
Bromine-79		X	
Bromine-81		X	
Cadmium-106		X	
Cadmium-108		X	
Cadmium-109	X		
Cadmium-110		X	
Cadmium-111		X	
Cadmium-112		X	

Isotope	Radioisotope	Stable isotope	Provided by NNSA
Cadmium-113		X	
Cadmium-114		X	
Cadmium-116		X	
Calcium-40		X	
Calcium-42		X	
Calcium-43		X	
Calcium-44		X	
Calcium-46		X	
Calcium-48		X	
Californium-249	X		
Californium-252	X		
Carbon-12		X	
Cerium-136		X	
Cerium-138		X	
Cerium-140		X	
Cerium-142		X	
Chlorine-35		X	
Chlorine-37		X	
Chromium-50		X	
Chromium-52		X	
Chromium-53		X	
Chromium-54		X	
Cobalt-60	X		
Copper-63		X	
Copper-65		X	
Copper-67	X		
Curium-244	X		X
Curium-248	X		X
Dysprosium-156		X	
Dysprosium-158		X	
Dysprosium-160		X	
Dysprosium-161		X	
Dysprosium-162		X	
Dysprosium-163		X	
Dysprosium-164		X	
Dysprosium-166	X		
Erbium-162		X	

Isotope	Radioisotope	Stable isotope	Provided by NNSA
Erbium-164		X	
Erbium-166		X	
Erbium-167		X	
Erbium-168		X	
Erbium-170		X	
Europium-151		X	
Europium-153		X	
Gadolinium-148	X		
Gadolinium-152		X	
Gadolinium-154		X	
Gadolinium-155		X	
Gadolinium-156		X	
Gadolinium-157		X	
Gadolinium-158		X	
Gadolinium-160		X	
Gallium-69		X	
Gallium-71		X	
Germanium-68	X		
Germanium-70		X	
Germanium-72		X	
Germanium-73		X	
Germanium-74		X	
Germanium-76		X	
Gold-199	X		
Hafnium-174		X	
Hafnium-176		X	
Hafnium-177		X	
Hafnium-178		X	
Hafnium-179		X	
Hafnium-180		X	
Helium-3		X	X
Holmium-166	X		
Indium-113		X	
Indium-115		X	
Iridium-191		X	
Iridium-192	X		
Iridium-193		X	

Isotope	Radioisotope	Stable isotope	Provided by NNSA
Iron-52	X		
Iron-54		X	
Iron-55	X		
Iron-56		X	
Iron-57		X	
Iron-58		X	
Krypton-78		X	
Krypton-80		X	
Krypton-82		X	
Krypton-84		X	
Krypton-86		X	
Lanthanum-138		X	
Lanthanum-139		X	
Lead-204		X	
Lead-206		X	
Lead-207		X	
Lead-208		X	
Lithium-6		X	X
Lithium-7		X	X
Lutetium-175		X	
Lutetium-176		X	
Lutetium-177	X		
Magnesium-24		X	
Magnesium-25		X	
Magnesium-26		X	
Magnesium-28	X		
Mercury-196		X	
Mercury-198		X	
Mercury-199		X	
Mercury-200		X	
Mercury-201		X	
Mercury-202		X	
Mercury-204		X	
Molybdenum-92		X	
Molybdenum-94		X	
Molybdenum-95		X	
Molybdenum-96		X	

Isotope	Radioisotope	Stable isotope	Provided by NNSA
Molybdenum-97		X	
Molybdenum-98		X	
Molybdenum-100		X	
Neodymium-142		X	
Neodymium-143		X	
Neodymium-144		X	
Neodymium-145		X	
Neodymium-146		X	
Neodymium-148		X	
Neodymium-150		X	
Neon-22		X	
Nickel-58		X	
Nickel-60		X	
Nickel-61		X	
Nickel-62		X	
Nickel-63	X		
Nickel-64		X	
Nitrogen-15		X	
Osmium-184		X	
Osmium-186		X	
Osmium-187		X	
Osmium-188		X	
Osmium-189		X	
Osmium-190		X	
Osmium-192		X	
Oxygen-16		X	
Palladium-102		X	
Palladium-104		X	
Palladium-105		X	
Palladium-106		X	
Palladium-108		X	
Palladium-110		X	
Platinum-190		X	
Platinum-192		X	
Platinum-194		X	
Platinum-195		X	
Platinum-196		X	

Isotope	Radioisotope	Stable isotope	Provided by NNSA
Platinum-198		X	
Plutonium-238	X		X
Plutonium-239	X		
Plutonium-240	X		
Plutonium-241	X		
Plutonium-242	X		X
Polonium-209	X		
Potassium-39		X	
Potassium-40		X	
Potassium-41		X	
Radium-223	X		
Radium-225	X		
Rhenium-185		X	
Rhenium-186	X		
Rhenium-187		X	
Rubidium-83	X		
Rubidium-85		X	
Rubidium-87		X	
Ruthenium-96		X	
Ruthenium-97	X		
Ruthenium-98		X	
Ruthenium-99		X	
Ruthenium-100		X	
Ruthenium-101		X	
Ruthenium-102		X	
Ruthenium-104		X	
Samarium-144		X	
Samarium-147		X	
Samarium-148		X	
Samarium-149		X	
Samarium-150		X	
Samarium-152		X	
Samarium-153	X		
Samarium-154		X	
Selenium-72	X		
Selenium-74		X	
Selenium-75	X		

Isotope	Radioisotope	Stable isotope	Provided by NNSA
Selenium-76		X	
Selenium-77		X	
Selenium-78		X	
Selenium-80		X	
Selenium-82		X	
Silicon-28		X	
Silicon-29		X	
Silicon-30		X	
Silicon-32	X		
Silver-107		X	
Silver-109		X	
Sodium-22	X		
Strontium-82	X		
Strontium-84		X	
Strontium-85	X		
Strontium-86		X	
Strontium-87		X	
Strontium-88		X	
Strontium-90	X		
Sulfur-32		X	
Sulfur-33		X	
Sulfur-34		X	
Sulfur-36		X	
Tantalum-180		X	
Tantalum-181		X	
Technetium-95	X		
Technetium-96	X		
Technetium-99	X		
Tellurium-120		X	
Tellurium-122		X	
Tellurium-123		X	
Tellurium-123[a]	X		
Tellurium-124		X	
Tellurium-125		X	
Tellurium-126		X	
Tellurium-128		X	
Tellurium-130		X	

Isotope	Radioisotope	Stable isotope	Provided by NNSA
Thallium-203		X	
Thallium-205		X	
Thorium-227	X		
Thorium-228	X		
Tin-112		X	
Tin-114		X	
Tin-115		X	
Tin-116		X	
Tin-117		X	
Tin-117[a]	X		
Tin-118		X	
Tin-119		X	
Tin-120		X	
Tin-122		X	
Tin-124		X	
Titanium-44	X		
Titanium-46		X	
Titanium-47		X	
Titanium-48		X	
Titanium-49		X	
Titanium-50		X	
Tungsten-180		X	
Tungsten-182		X	
Tungsten-183		X	
Tungsten-184		X	
Tungsten-186		X	
Tungsten-188	X		
Uranium-234	X		
Uranium-235	X		X
Uranium-238	X		X
Vanadium-48	X		
Vanadium-49	X		
Vanadium-50		X	
Xenon-124		X	
Xenon-126		X	
Xenon-127	X		
Xenon-129		X	

Isotope	Radioisotope	Stable isotope	Provided by NNSA
Xenon-131		X	
Xenon-134		X	
Xenon-136		X	
Ytterbium-168		X	
Ytterbium-170		X	
Ytterbium-171		X	
Ytterbium-172		X	
Ytterbium-173		X	
Ytterbium-174		X	
Ytterbium-176		X	
Yttrium-88	X		
Zinc-64		X	
Zinc-65	X		
Zinc-66		X	
Zinc-67		X	
Zinc-68		X	
Zinc-70		X	
Zirconium-88	X		
Zirconium-90		X	
Zirconium-91		X	
Zirconium-92		X	
Zirconium-94		X	
Zirconium-96		X	

Source: DOE.

[a]Tellurium-123 and tin-117 each has two forms offered by the Isotope Program, one that is stable and a second that emits radiation when it decays to the stable state.

Appendix II: Comments from the Department of Energy

Department of Energy
Office of Science
Washington, DC 20585

Office of the Director

May 14, 2012

Mr. Gene Aloise
Director, Natural Resources and Environment
Government Accountability Office
441 G Street
Washington, DC 20548

Dear Mr. Aloise:

Thank you for the opportunity to comment on the draft Government Accountability
Office (GAO) report entitled, "Managing Critical Isotopes: DOE's Isotope Program
Needs Better Planning for Setting Prices and Managing Production Risks" (GAO-12-
591). We have reviewed the draft report and provide general comments below as well as
substantive and technical/editorial comments as an attachment. The comments provided
here have been coordinated with other relevant offices of the Department of Energy
(DOE).

The GAO was charged by the Energy and Environment and the Investigations and
Oversight Subcommittees of the House Committee on Science, Space, and Technology
"to determine (1) which isotopes are produced, sold or distributed either by the Isotope
Program or NNSA [National Nuclear Security Administration] and how the two agencies
make isotopes available for commercial and research applications; (2) what steps the
Isotope Program takes to provide isotopes for commercial and research applications; and
(3) the extent to which DOE is assessing and mitigating risks facing the Isotope
Program." We recognize that conducting a review of the Department's isotope activities
is an enormous undertaking, and in particular, we appreciate the time and thoroughness
the GAO took to review the Department's program.

The Isotope Program was transferred from the Office of Nuclear Energy to the Office of
Nuclear Physics within the Office of Science late in FY 2009. Over the past couple of
years, the Office of Nuclear Physics has taken several actions and made significant
changes in the Isotope Program, and they should be recognized for their extensive efforts
over such a short period of time. These efforts include implementing a new federal
management structure, creating the National Isotope Development Center to improve
relations with stakeholders, conducting strategic planning with federal advisory
committees and stakeholders to develop priorities, organizing workshops with federal
agencies to better understand demand, establishing a research and development program
to create new and improved isotope production techniques, updating costing and pricing
procedures to lower costs and update prices, and incorporating new production sites into
the program to increase isotope availability. While a great deal of progress has been
made, we acknowledge that our plans to improve the effectiveness of the Isotope

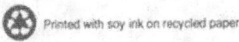
Printed with soy ink on recycled paper

Program are not yet complete. Most notably, the Isotope Program is now in the process of developing a federal strategic plan that incorporates input from a number of the strategic exercises that we have been conducting over the past couple of years.

There are several statements in the report that the Department does not find to be accurate characterizations of the Isotope Program. First, contrary to the Isotope Program, NNSA does not have the mission to supply isotopes to stakeholders. NNSA is a source of isotopes to the Isotope Program should they be available for distribution out of their material stockpiles, not a supplier of isotopes directly to consumers. Second, the report states that the Isotope Program has not fully assessed the pricing of most of these isotopes. The Isotope Program expends considerable effort in establishing prices, including full bottom-up activity-based costing for isotope production, interactions with the isotope user community, and negotiations with isotope customers. Likewise, the "value of isotopes to customers" has always been considered in pricing development.

A concerning theme throughout the report, and related to the first recommendation, is the maximization of revenue and the suggestion that greater emphasis should be placed on setting prices to increase revenue generated by the program. The Isotope Program is a complex program that provides isotopes for both commercial customers and for research purposes, requiring different approaches to setting prices. The Isotope Program generally sets prices to fulfill the mandate established by the Atomic Energy Act of 1954 to provide isotopes at prices that do not discourage their use. For commercial customers, prices are set in accordance with market prices when such prices exceed production costs. To help inform its price setting practices, the Isotope Program has initiated two marketing studies that will provide input into the assessment of market prices, supplementing the market evaluations that are inherent in annually setting isotope prices and negotiating contracts.

The Department has the following general comments regarding each of the recommendations.

Recommendation 1: "Clearly define the factors to be considered when it sets prices for isotopes sold commercially, including defining under what circumstances it will set prices at or above full cost recovery. This should include assessing when appropriate, current information on the value of the isotope to the customer and the price of similar products."

The factors considered when the Isotope Program sets prices are articulated in the 1990 Pricing Policy Memo, which was shared with the GAO at the beginning of the audit. The updated 2012 Pricing Policy, which is currently being finalized by the Department and of which a draft was shared with the GAO, also identifies the factors considered by the Isotope Program when establishing prices. These factors do include the value of the isotope to the customer.

Recommendation 2 "In conjunction with strategic planning efforts already underway, the Isotope Program should create clear goals and objectives to serve as

a basis for a risk assessment, identify risks to achieving its goals and objectives, and determine what actions to take to manage risks."

While the Department believes that the Isotope Program has established clear goals and objectives, the federal strategic plan currently under development will provide better clarity of these goals and objectives and the Program intends to develop a programmatic risk management document.

Recommendation 3 "Consolidate and prioritize the lists of high-priority isotopes so that the program can better focus its resources on the highest priorities."

These lists of isotopes developed through separate processes represent very different categories of isotopes, with very different paths for production or availability. As such, they may not directly compete for resources. While a consolidated list is possible (although categories will still be needed), the Department will need to assess the value added of doing an overall prioritization as there are many paths of isotopes that can be considered in parallel. In addition, while these lists or categories of isotopes provide overall guidance in terms of priority for the Isotope Program, decisions regarding investments are also largely driven by merit-based peer review. The report does not adequately address or recognize the role and importance that peer review mechanisms have on making funding decisions. Just because an isotope is high priority for the community does not guarantee that there is an entity that has developed a compelling and credible approach to producing it.

Recommendation 4 "Establish clear guidance for managing the Isotope Program's revolving fund."

This is a sound recommendation, but one that can only be addressed after the completion of the federal strategic plan, which is underway.

Thank you, again, for the opportunity to provide comment on this draft. We look forward to receiving your final report. If you have any questions related to this letter, please feel free to contact Dr. Jehanne Gillo at (301) 903-1455.

Sincerely,

W. F. Brinkman
Director, Office of Science

Attachment

Appendix III: GAO Contact and Staff Acknowledgments

GAO Contact

Gene Aloise, (202) 512-3841 or aloisee@gao.gov

Staff Acknowledgments

In addition to the individual named above, Ned H. Woodward, Assistant Director; Wyatt R. Hundrup; Katherine Killebrew; and Michael Krafve made key contributions to this report. Eric Bachhuber, Ellen W. Chu, R. Scott Fletcher, Cindy Gilbert, Jonathan Kucskar, Mehrzad Nadji, and Timothy M. Persons also made important contributions.

GAO's Mission	The Government Accountability Office, the audit, evaluation, and investigative arm of Congress, exists to support Congress in meeting its constitutional responsibilities and to help improve the performance and accountability of the federal government for the American people. GAO examines the use of public funds; evaluates federal programs and policies; and provides analyses, recommendations, and other assistance to help Congress make informed oversight, policy, and funding decisions. GAO's commitment to good government is reflected in its core values of accountability, integrity, and reliability.
Obtaining Copies of GAO Reports and Testimony	The fastest and easiest way to obtain copies of GAO documents at no cost is through GAO's website (www.gao.gov). Each weekday afternoon, GAO posts on its website newly released reports, testimony, and correspondence. To have GAO e-mail you a list of newly posted products, go to www.gao.gov and select "E-mail Updates."
Order by Phone	The price of each GAO publication reflects GAO's actual cost of production and distribution and depends on the number of pages in the publication and whether the publication is printed in color or black and white. Pricing and ordering information is posted on GAO's website, http://www.gao.gov/ordering.htm. Place orders by calling (202) 512-6000, toll free (866) 801-7077, or TDD (202) 512-2537. Orders may be paid for using American Express, Discover Card, MasterCard, Visa, check, or money order. Call for additional information.
Connect with GAO	Connect with GAO on Facebook, Flickr, Twitter, and YouTube. Subscribe to our RSS Feeds or E-mail Updates. Listen to our Podcasts. Visit GAO on the web at www.gao.gov.
To Report Fraud, Waste, and Abuse in Federal Programs	Contact: Website: www.gao.gov/fraudnet/fraudnet.htm E-mail: fraudnet@gao.gov Automated answering system: (800) 424-5454 or (202) 512-7470
Congressional Relations	Katherine Siggerud, Managing Director, siggerudk@gao.gov, (202) 512-4400, U.S. Government Accountability Office, 441 G Street NW, Room 7125, Washington, DC 20548
Public Affairs	Chuck Young, Managing Director, youngc1@gao.gov, (202) 512-4800 U.S. Government Accountability Office, 441 G Street NW, Room 7149 Washington, DC 20548

Please Print on Recycled Paper.

www.ingramcontent.com/pod-product-compliance
Lightning Source LLC
Chambersburg PA
CBHW080922290526
45795CB00007BA/2625